THE MANAGING CASHFLOW POCKETBOOK

By Anne Hawkins and Clive Turner

Drawings by Phil Hailstone

"Managers do not understand the difference between profit and cash. This book explains the issues involved clearly and simply. It is an essential guide for the non-financially trained manager."
Nick Bacon, Director, Lloyds TSB Development Capital Ltd

"An invaluable guide to the most critical of business issues – easy to read and full of helpful ideas." **J. B. McCarthy, Financial Director, Triton plc**

CONTENTS

1 INTRODUCTION

MANAGING CASH

People have always had
to manage cash.

It is just the same with businesses.

INTRODUCTION

WHAT IS CASH?

What do accountants mean by cash?

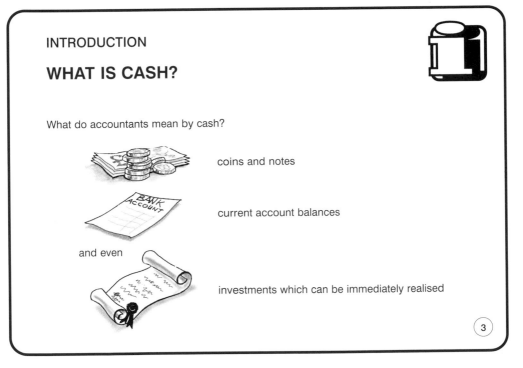

coins and notes

current account balances

and even

investments which can be immediately realised

INTRODUCTION

USES OF CASH

Why do we need it?

To pay:

- Suppliers - for materials, services and equipment
- Employees - for their services
- Lenders - interest
- Investors - dividends
- Government - tax

MEDIUM OF EXCHANGE

Gone are the days of bartering:

Cash is the **medium of exchange.**
Without it we cannot acquire materials
or add value.

What happens if we do not have it?

The business will grind to a halt
resulting in **INSOLVENCY!**
... leading to bankruptcy or liquidation.

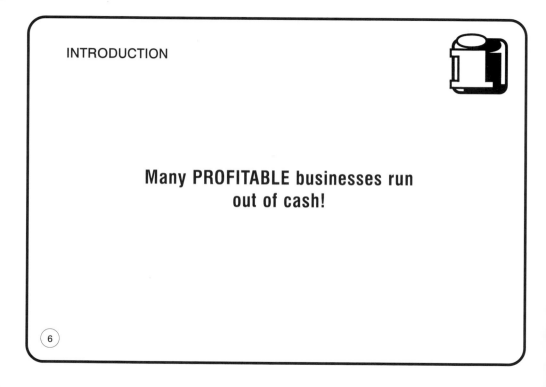

**Many PROFITABLE businesses run
out of cash!**

MANAGING CASH

MANAGING CASH

GETTING IT RIGHT

Which means:
'Managing the cashflows into and
out of the business in order to have
the right amount of cash available at
the right time'.

CASHFLOW

Cash movements are measured in terms of cashflow.

IN - from customers, investments   RECEIPTS

OUT - to suppliers, employees, lenders,   PAYMENTS
investors, government

Managing cash requires these flows to be **PLANNED**:

- How much?

- Will cash flow **IN** or **OUT**?

- **WHEN** will it flow?

Cash flows are reported in the internal Cashflow Statement.

CASHFLOW STATEMENT

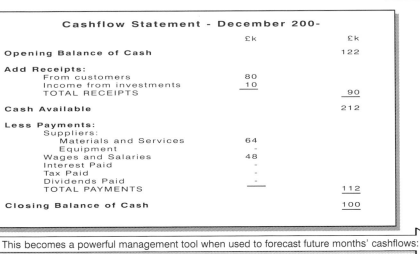

Cashflow Statement - December 200-		
	£k	£k
Opening Balance of Cash		122
Add Receipts:		
From customers	80	
Income from investments	10	
TOTAL RECEIPTS		90
Cash Available		212
Less Payments:		
Suppliers:		
Materials and Services	64	
Equipment	-	
Wages and Salaries	48	
Interest Paid	-	
Tax Paid	-	
Dividends Paid	-	
TOTAL PAYMENTS		112
Closing Balance of Cash		100

(10) This becomes a powerful management tool when used to forecast future months' cashflows:

CASHFLOW FORECASTS

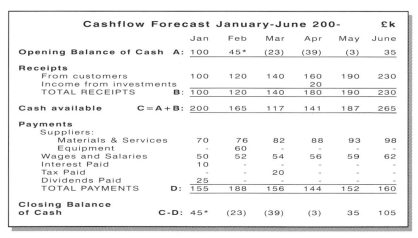

Cashflow Forecast January-June 200-						£k
	Jan	Feb	Mar	Apr	May	June
Opening Balance of Cash A:	100	45*	(23)	(39)	(3)	35
Receipts						
From customers	100	120	140	160	190	230
Income from investments				20		
TOTAL RECEIPTS B:	100	120	140	180	190	230
Cash available C = A + B:	200	165	117	141	187	265
Payments						
Suppliers:						
Materials & Services	70	76	82	88	93	98
Equipment	-	60	-	-	-	-
Wages and Salaries	50	52	54	56	59	62
Interest Paid	10	-	-	-	-	-
Tax Paid	-	-	20	-	-	-
Dividends Paid	25	-	-	-	-	-
TOTAL PAYMENTS D:	155	188	156	144	152	160
Closing Balance of Cash C - D:	45*	(23)	(39)	(3)	35	105

Note that the closing balance for Jan is the opening balance for Feb and so on.

FOREWARNED IS FOREARMED

- Cashflow must be **managed**, not just allowed to happen

- Forewarned is forearmed

The forecast (page 11) gives advanced warning of the cash problems from February until April, so the business can respond, eg:

Increase Receipts:

- Offer customers discount for early payment
- Sell extra units from stock
- Factor sales invoices

Reduce Payments:

- Defer the purchase of equipment
- Reschedule material purchases by reducing stock
- Negotiate extended credit from suppliers

PLAN OR PANIC

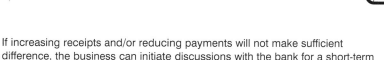

- If increasing receipts and/or reducing payments will not make sufficient difference, the business can initiate discussions with the bank for a short-term overdraft facility, well ahead of when it is required

Without the forecast there would have been confusion and panic as the growing business ran out of cash ... **NOT** the way to impress your bank manager!

(13)

NOTES

PROFIT VERSUS CASH

PROFIT IS NOT CASH

"My business is profitable. Why should I have to worry about cash?"

Because many profitable businesses run out of cash!
PROFIT $\neq$ CASH

PROFIT VERSUS CASH

PROFIT IS NOT CASH

What is 'Profit'?

- Profit is made when we sell a product or service for more than it cost to produce,
  ie: Sales less Attributable Cost = Operating Profit

- Profit is assessed when the business makes the sale - **NOT** when the customer pays

What is 'Cash'?

- Cash is generated when the cash inflows (Receipts) exceed
  the cash outflows (Payments)

PROFIT IS NOT CASH

PROFIT equals **SALES** less **ATTRIBUTABLE COSTS**

BUT

SALES is the Value of products or services sold during the period

NOT Cash received from customers

ATTRIBUTABLE COSTS are the Costs incurred in manufacturing and distributing the products or services that have been **sold**

NOT Cash paid to suppliers and employees

(18)

So ... **PROFIT DOES NOT EQUAL CASH**

BUSINESS FLOWS

Note how goods and services flow at different times, and in the opposite direction, to cash.

Flow of:

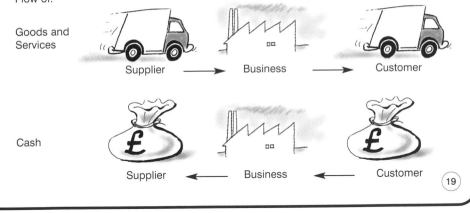

| | Supplier | → | Business | → | Customer |

Goods and Services — Supplier → Business → Customer

Cash — Supplier ← Business ← Customer

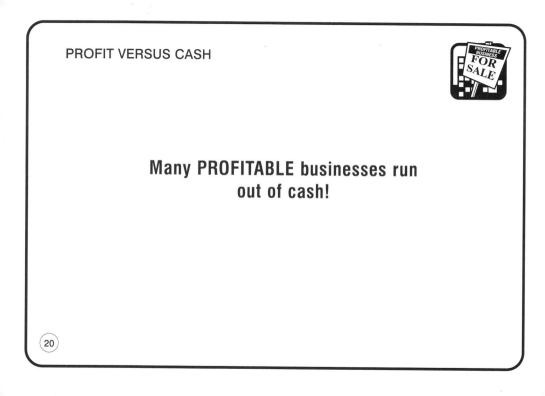

**Many PROFITABLE businesses run
out of cash!**

RECONCILIATION
OF PROFIT TO CASH

THE LINK

"Whilst I can appreciate that Profit and Cashflow are measured in different ways, there must surely be some link?"

Yes, there is.

It is all a question of **TIMING**.

RECONCILIATION OF PROFIT TO CASH

EXAMPLE

THE MARKET STALL

A man is in business selling cabbages. In the morning he sets out with £100 in his pocket which he uses to buy 500 cabbages at 20p each from the wholesaler.

He sells all 500 cabbages at the street corner for 50p each and goes home a happy man.

- How much **PROFIT** has he made?

Sales (500 @ 50p)	£250
Attributable Cost (500 @ 20p)	£100
Operating Profit	£150

- How much **CASH** has he generated?

Opening Cash	£100
Payments (500 @ 20p)	£100
Cash available	£ NIL
Receipts (500 @ 50p)	£250
Closing cash	£250
Cash Generated	£150

RECONCILIATION OF PROFIT TO CASH

EXAMPLE

THE MARKET STALL

Operating Profit	£150
Cash Generated	£150

Why are the two the same?

Because there are no TIMING differences.

- Sales = Receipts - because customers do not take credit

- Costs = Payments - because there is no credit from the wholesaler
  - because the cabbage seller does not keep stock

Most businesses are involved in giving and taking credit and holding stock and must therefore build these timing differences into any reconciliation of Profit and Cash.

RECONCILIATION OF PROFIT TO CASH

EXAMPLE

THE SUPERMARKET

What happens, for example, if our cabbage seller sells his cabbages to a supermarket chain, which takes 60 days credit?

He uses his £100 cash
to buy the cabbages

... sells them

... but then has to wait 60 days for his money!

He makes the same profit, but has no money for more cabbages until the customer pays.

RECONCILIATION OF PROFIT TO CASH

TIMING

Example

- A business buys materials in March which it converts into a product, which is delivered to the customer the same month
- The supplier allows 90 days credit
- The customer pays in 60 days

Business Flows

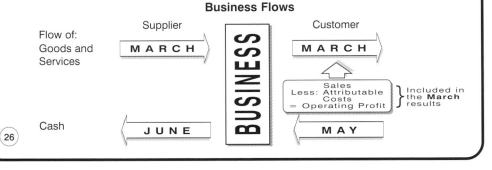

RECONCILIATION OF PROFIT TO CASH

TIMING

- How do the business flows operate in your organisation?

    - How much credit do your suppliers give you?
    - How long does it take to produce the product?
    - How much credit do you give your customers?

- Who manages these flows?
- Credit given and taken must be **negotiated**
- Improved material flows will impact on lead times and cash

COULD YOU DO IT BETTER?
(See page 73 onwards for useful tips)

RECONCILIATION STATEMENT

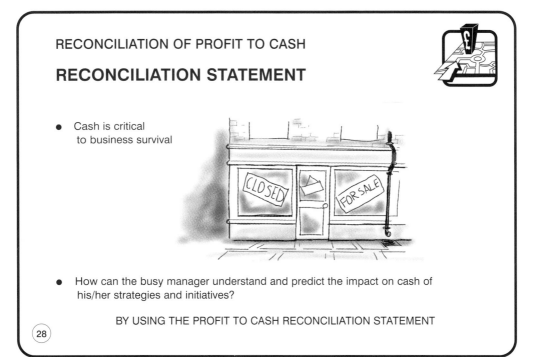

- Cash is critical to business survival

- How can the busy manager understand and predict the impact on cash of his/her strategies and initiatives?

BY USING THE PROFIT TO CASH RECONCILIATION STATEMENT

RECONCILIATION STATEMENT

- The Reconciliation of Profit to Cash Statement reconciles Operating Profit to Net Cashflow, adjusting transactions from a 'Profit' perspective to a cashflow basis

PROFIT

CASHFLOW

- Operating Profit equals Sales less Attributable Costs
- Net Cashflow is the difference between opening and closing cash balances for the period

RECONCILIATION OF PROFIT TO CASH

RECONCILIATION STATEMENT

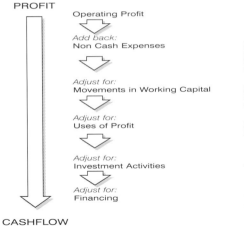

PROFIT

Operating Profit

Add back:
Non Cash Expenses

Depreciation
Stock Reserve
Warranty Provision
Bad Debt Provision

Adjust for:
Movements in Working Capital

Stock
Debtors
Creditors

Adjust for:
Uses of Profit

Interest
Dividend
Tax

Adjust for:
Investment Activities

Capital Expenditure

Adjust for:
Financing

Changes to Share Capital
and Loan Capital

CASHFLOW

Cash generated/consumed

The following pages explain each step of the reconciliation process.

RECONCILIATION STATEMENT

OPERATING PROFIT

Operating Profit

Add back:
Depreciation

Inc/Dec in Stock
Inc/Dec in Debtors
Inc/Dec in Creditors

Interest Paid/Received
Dividend Paid

Tax Paid

Capital Expenditure

Inc/Dec Share Capital
Inc/Dec Loan Capital

NET CASHFLOW

Operating profit

- Operating Profit is measured when products or services are sold to customers

- This will result in a cash inflow when the customer pays

RECONCILIATION OF PROFIT TO CASH

RECONCILIATION STATEMENT

DEPRECIATION

Operating Profit

⇩

Add back:
Depreciation

⇩

Inc/Dec in Stock
Inc/Dec in Debtors
Inc/Dec in Creditors

⇩

Interest Paid/Received
Dividend Paid

⇩

Tax Paid

⇩

Capital Expenditure

⇩

Inc/Dec Share Capital
Inc/Dec Loan Capital

⇩

NET CASHFLOW

Depreciation

- Depreciation is a charge against **profits** made to ensure that the cost of an investment in, eg: new equipment, is spread over its useful life

- There is no cash outflow (no purchase invoice) for depreciation - it is what accountants call a non cash expense

- The **cash** has already been paid out at the moment of purchase

- As part of the process of reconciling profit to cash you therefore need to add it back to Operating Profit

RECONCILIATION STATEMENT

STOCKS

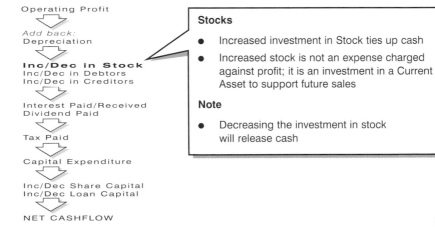

Operating Profit

Add back:
Depreciation

Inc/Dec in Stock
Inc/Dec in Debtors
Inc/Dec in Creditors

Interest Paid/Received
Dividend Paid

Tax Paid

Capital Expenditure

Inc/Dec Share Capital
Inc/Dec Loan Capital

NET CASHFLOW

Stocks

- Increased investment in Stock ties up cash
- Increased stock is not an expense charged against profit; it is an investment in a Current Asset to support future sales

Note

- Decreasing the investment in stock will release cash

33

RECONCILIATION STATEMENT

DEBTORS

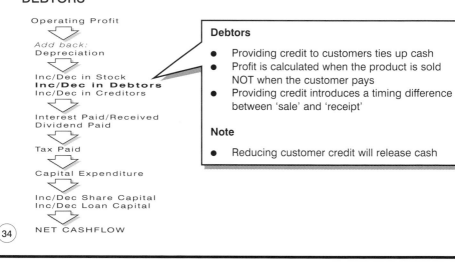

Operating Profit

Add back:
Depreciation

Inc/Dec in Stock
Inc/Dec in Debtors
Inc/Dec in Creditors

Interest Paid/Received
Dividend Paid

Tax Paid

Capital Expenditure

Inc/Dec Share Capital
Inc/Dec Loan Capital

NET CASHFLOW

Debtors

- Providing credit to customers ties up cash
- Profit is calculated when the product is sold NOT when the customer pays
- Providing credit introduces a timing difference between 'sale' and 'receipt'

Note

- Reducing customer credit will release cash

RECONCILIATION STATEMENT

CREDITORS

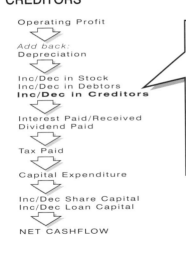

Operating Profit

Add back:
Depreciation

Inc/Dec in Stock
Inc/Dec in Debtors
Inc/Dec in Creditors

Interest Paid/Received
Dividend Paid

Tax Paid

Capital Expenditure

Inc/Dec Share Capital
Inc/Dec Loan Capital

NET CASHFLOW

Creditors

- When the business makes a sale, the goods and services used are charged against profit; whether the business has paid for them or not!

- An increase in creditors means the business is using more of its suppliers' money and keeping its own longer

- Purchasing on credit enables businesses to produce products whilst keeping cash intact

RECONCILIATION STATEMENT

INTEREST, TAX AND DIVIDENDS

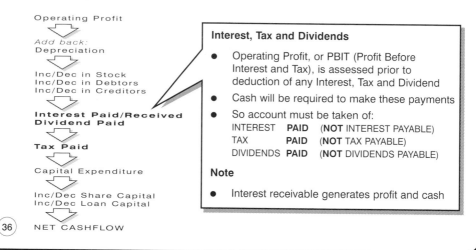

Operating Profit

⇩

Add back:
Depreciation

⇩

Inc/Dec in Stock
Inc/Dec in Debtors
Inc/Dec in Creditors

⇩

Interest Paid/Received
Dividend Paid

⇩

Tax Paid

⇩

Capital Expenditure

⇩

Inc/Dec Share Capital
Inc/Dec Loan Capital

⇩

NET CASHFLOW

Interest, Tax and Dividends

- Operating Profit, or PBIT (Profit Before Interest and Tax), is assessed prior to deduction of any Interest, Tax and Dividend

- Cash will be required to make these payments

- So account must be taken of:
  INTEREST **PAID** (**NOT** INTEREST PAYABLE)
  TAX **PAID** (**NOT** TAX PAYABLE)
  DIVIDENDS **PAID** (**NOT** DIVIDENDS PAYABLE)

Note

- Interest receivable generates profit and cash

RECONCILIATION STATEMENT

CAPITAL EXPENDITURE

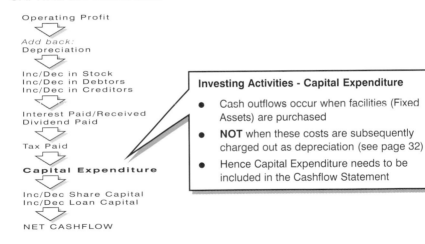

Operating Profit

Add back:
Depreciation

Inc/Dec in Stock
Inc/Dec in Debtors
Inc/Dec in Creditors

Interest Paid/Received
Dividend Paid

Tax Paid

Capital Expenditure

Inc/Dec Share Capital
Inc/Dec Loan Capital

NET CASHFLOW

Investing Activities - Capital Expenditure

- Cash outflows occur when facilities (Fixed Assets) are purchased

- **NOT** when these costs are subsequently charged out as depreciation (see page 32)

- Hence Capital Expenditure needs to be included in the Cashflow Statement

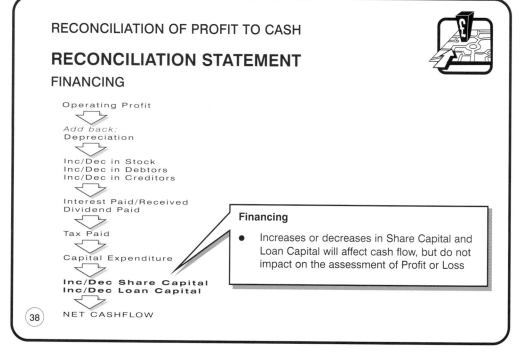

RECONCILIATION OF PROFIT TO CASH

RECONCILIATION STATEMENT

FINANCING

Operating Profit

Add back:
Depreciation

Inc/Dec in Stock
Inc/Dec in Debtors
Inc/Dec in Creditors

Interest Paid/Received
Dividend Paid

Tax Paid

Capital Expenditure

**Inc/Dec Share Capital
Inc/Dec Loan Capital**

NET CASHFLOW

Financing

- Increases or decreases in Share Capital and Loan Capital will affect cash flow, but do not impact on the assessment of Profit or Loss

38

RECONCILIATION OF PROFIT TO CASH

RECONCILIATION STATEMENT

- Operating Profit has now been adjusted to Net Cashflow

- This is reconciled to the movement in cash:

		£
Less:	Opening Cash/(Bank Overdraft)	xx
	Closing Cash/(Bank Overdraft)	xx
=	NET CASH (INFLOW)/OUTFLOW	xx

- The completed format of the report is shown on page 40

Note: *The figures used in the Reconciliation Statement are from the detailed example contained in Appendix Three.*

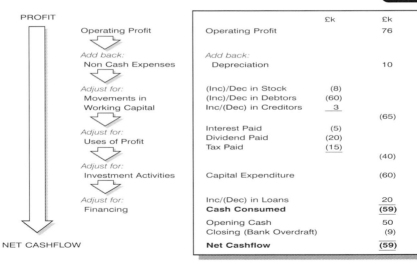

RECONCILIATION OF PROFIT TO CASH

RECONCILIATION STATEMENT

PROFIT

Operating Profit

Add back:
Non Cash Expenses

Adjust for:
Movements in
Working Capital

Adjust for:
Uses of Profit

Adjust for:
Investment Activities

Adjust for:
Financing

NET CASHFLOW

	£k	£k
Operating Profit		76
Add back:		
Depreciation		10
(Inc)/Dec in Stock	(8)	
(Inc)/Dec in Debtors	(60)	
Inc/(Dec) in Creditors	3	
		(65)
Interest Paid	(5)	
Dividend Paid	(20)	
Tax Paid	(15)	
		(40)
Capital Expenditure		(60)
Inc/(Dec) in Loans		20
Cash Consumed		**(59)**
Opening Cash		50
Closing (Bank Overdraft)		(9)
Net Cashflow		**(59)**

IMPROVING CASHFLOW

PAYING FOR EXPANSION

- The Reconciliation Statement on page 40 reconciles Operating Profit to net cashflow

- Note the irony:

    EXPANDING businesses, needing Capital Expenditure, increased stocks and higher levels of debtors, will normally **CONSUME** cash

    CONTRACTING businesses ... no longer investing in new facilities and with reducing levels of stocks and debtors will normally **GENERATE** cash

Hence as the successful business expands, it is more at risk of insolvency!

OPERATING PROFIT

So what steps can be taken to **MANAGE** cashflow rather than just letting it happen? Consider each aspect of the Reconciliation Statement in turn.

- **To improve cashflow: Increase Operating Profit**

- Operating Profit is the difference between Sales and Attributable Cost

- To improve Operating Profit we need to:

  - Increase Sales (of profitable products!)

  or

  - Maintain Sales whilst decreasing costs

OPERATING PROFIT

Aim: Increase Sales

- Increase Sales Volume
    - benefits of economies of scale
    - utilising excess capacity

- Increase selling prices
    - usually the simplest option
    - what will be the impact on sales volume? KNOW YOUR MARKETS!

- Manage the sales mix
    - communicate and prioritise high profit earners
    - often businesses achieve the sales level but miss the profit target

Aim: Maintain Sales whilst decreasing costs

- Improve material purchasing
- Reduce scrap and other `wastage' of resources

- Increase labour efficiency
- Reduce overheads

DEPRECIATION

DOES NOT RESULT IN CASH OUTFLOWS!

Therefore, increasing or decreasing the charge for Depreciation will not affect the cash position!

Remember:

Depreciation is included as a cost in calculating Operating Profit but is then 'added back' in the cashflow statement (page 32).

IMPROVING CASHFLOW

WORKING CAPITAL
STOCKS/DEBTORS/CREDITORS

- **To improve Cashflow:** **Decrease Stock**
   Decrease Debtors
   Increase Creditors

BUT NOTE opposite movements will consume cash!

These issues are discussed in detail in a subsequent section, Managing Working Capital.

IMPROVING CASHFLOW

INTEREST PAID

■ **To improve cashflow: Reduce interest paid**

Interest paid is determined by:

● Amount borrowed
● Rate charged

Hence: **AIM TO MINIMISE BORROWINGS**
              AIM TO MINIMISE RATES

IMPROVING CASHFLOW

INTEREST PAID

Aim: Minimise Borrowings

- Self-financing
  - If possible reduce Loan Capital or the Bank Overdraft through **self-financing**, by generating and retaining profit

- Eliminate surplus investment
  - Every £1 invested in the business has to come from somewhere
    ie: Use of Funds equals Source of Funds
    Net Assets Employed equals Net Capital Employed
  - Loans form part of most companies' Source of Funds
  - Hence, by controlling Use of Funds, eg: eliminating surplus fixed assets and working capital, Source of Funds can be **reduced**, giving businesses the opportunity to reduce borrowings

A Business Financial Model explaining these concepts is developed in *'The Balance Sheet Pocketbook'*.

IMPROVING CASHFLOW

INTEREST PAID

Aim: Minimise Rates

- Most rates are charged at Base Rate + x%

- Whilst businesses can do little to influence Base Rate, the additional percentage charged is a reflection of the lender's perception of financial risk

- Perceived risk will be reduced where the business:
  - balances the Sources of Finance appropriately
  - presents a professional managerial approach
  - is seen to give emphasis to planning and forecasting

- Evaluate raising loans abroad if appropriate and interest rates are favourable

Note: the x% is negotiable!

TAX PAYMENTS

- **To improve cashflow: Reduce Tax paid**

- There are tax aspects to most business decisions

- Larger companies employ tax experts, others use their accountants or auditors

- Businesses - like individuals - aim to minimise their tax bills

TAX AVOIDANCE involves
running the business in a
tax-efficient manner.

However, TAX EVASION is
illegal and you are likely to
end up behind bars!

DIVIDEND PAYMENTS

- **To improve cashflow: Reduce Dividends Paid**

- Earnings are the profits left over for the shareholders once all costs have been met

- Shareholders seek two types of return from their investment:
  - Income, ie: Dividends
  - Growth, ie: increase in the value of their investment

- Some of the Earnings are used to pay dividends, the rest will be re-invested within the business to help provide growth

EARNINGS

DIVIDENDS   RETAINED PROFIT

DIVIDEND PAYMENTS

- The level of dividend declared is the result of a considered dividend policy to balance the Shareholders' expectation for Income and Growth

- Most companies would prefer to retain all available profits if this were feasible, therefore maximising funds available for reinvestment and avoiding a cash outflow

- Many companies offer extra shares in lieu of dividends as an alternative way of retaining the cash within the business

IMPROVING CASHFLOW

CAPITAL EXPENDITURE

- **To improve cashflow: Reduce or Reschedule Capital Expenditure**

- Companies need Processes/Facilities in order to produce their products or services

- Purchasing decisions are strategic - the choice determines how the business will produce its products/services for many years ahead

- Such decisions are, therefore, subject to scrutiny by top management

- Curtailing expenditure has implications on competitive advantage and the costs/benefits must be weighed carefully

- Consider other options, eg:
  - sub contract (if appropriate)
  - factor other manufacturers' products
  - short-term policy; maintenance not replacement
  - evaluate leasing options

IMPROVING CASHFLOW

FINANCING

- ■ **To improve cashflow: Increase Share Capital and Loans**

- ● Long-term finance must be appropriate to the needs of the business

- ● Too little (under-capitalisation) and the business will have on-going cashflow crises

- ● Too much (over-capitalisation) and the money will be invested inefficiently, resulting in poor levels of profitability

Note: Changes in Long-term funding will also affect the cash required to meet future interest and dividend payments

TRADE-OFFS

Most actions have more than one impact on cashflow.

Action	Trade-off	
Offer customers discount for early settlement	Brings in Cash from Debtors v	Reduces Profit* by the Discount
Increase Loan Capital	Brings Cash into the business v	Increased Interest Payments

* and remember Profit is part of the cashflow!

Evaluate the overall impact on the business

TIMING

Remember   Managing Cash is:
'Managing the cashflows into and out of the business in order to have the right amount of cash available **at the right time**'.

Will the proposed action result in the required cashflow **at the appropriate time?**

Collecting overdues from customers will bring cash in more quickly than selling surplus office space!

MANAGING
WORKING CAPITAL

MANAGING WORKING CAPITAL

INTRODUCTION

In most businesses efficient management of Working Capital is the key to successful cash management.

What is Working Capital?

- Businesses raise Long-term money (Source of Funds) in order to invest it in the business (Use of Funds)

- Investment is required to provide:
  - Facilities/Processes (Accountant's jargon: Fixed Assets)
  - Products/Services (Accountant's jargon: Working Capital)

These terms and the Working Capital cycle are explained in *The Balance Sheet Pocketbook*.

MANAGING WORKING CAPITAL

WHAT IS WORKING CAPITAL?

WORKING CAPITAL CYCLE

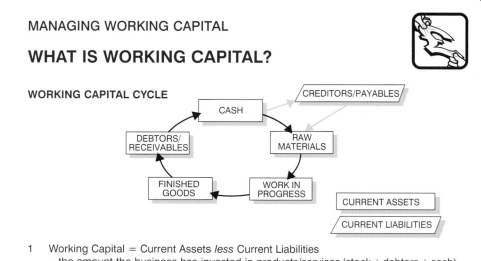

1. Working Capital = Current Assets *less* Current Liabilities
   - the amount the business has invested in products/services (stock + debtors + cash) less the value of goods and services owed to suppliers (creditors)

2. Stock = Raw Material + Work in Progress + Finished Goods

HOW MUCH WORKING CAPITAL IS REQUIRED?

This is a function of:

- The size of the business

- Credit given and taken

- Lead time through the manufacturing process

- Range of products/services offered

How much Working Capital does your business **need**?

How much Working Capital does it **have**?

MANAGING WORKING CAPITAL

HOW MUCH SHOULD I HAVE?

You should have as little Working Capital as possible, consistent with maximising business profitability!

The objectives are to complete the Working Capital Cycle:

1 As fast as possible

Why? - minimise the investment and hence improve the return
- reduce risk (see pages 62-3)

2 As frequently as possible

Why? - completing the cycle generates profit and cash

HOW MUCH WORKING CAPITAL?

REDUCING RISK

- There is only one part of the Current Asset cycle that accountants like
  - **CASH**; everything else represents risk

- When you use cash to buy Raw Material:
  - what if there is a modification?
  - what if the customer cancels?
  - does the material have a shelf life?
  - could you sell the material back or
    to someone else?

- When you convert Raw Material to Work in Progress
  and Finished Goods:
  - ditto

- Even when you despatch the goods:
  - what if the customer does not pay?

HOW MUCH WORKING CAPITAL?
REDUCING RISK

- The degree of risk is affected by the type of product and whether it is customer-specific

  However

  There is no benefit whatsoever to the business until the Working Capital Cycle has been completed and cash received from the customer

- Hence to persuade the accountant to part with cash and embark on the cycle, you must convince him/her that the return is worth the risk

- By reducing the time taken to complete the cycle, the risk can be reduced

MEASURING PERFORMANCE

RATIOS

- Ratios are used to express Working Capital management performance

- These ratios express each component of the cycle in terms of time (a number of days)

- Improvements in Working Capital management can then be seen by a reduction in the number of days required to complete the cycle

- Working Capital Days equals no. days Raw Material
  - *plus* no. days Work in Progress
  - *plus* no. days Finished Goods
  - *plus* no. days Debtors
  - *less* no. days Creditors

MEASURING PERFORMANCE

STOCK DAYS

● When calculating Stock days, look at the business as a series of flows of inputs and outputs:

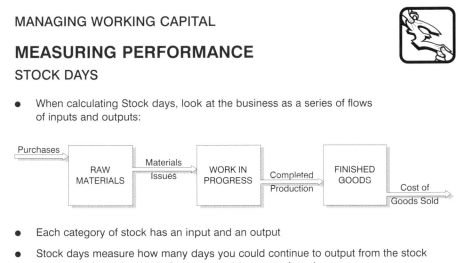

● Each category of stock has an input and an output

● Stock days measure how many days you could continue to output from the stock category, without inputs, before you would run out of stock

MEASURING PERFORMANCE

ADAPTING THE MODEL

NOTE: This model must be adapted to reflect the business:

eg: **Retailer with Centralised Warehousing**

eg: **Independent Retailer**

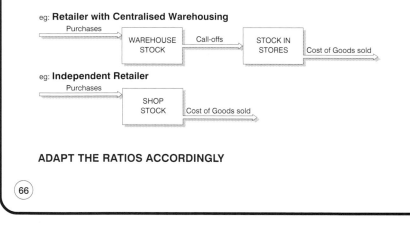

ADAPT THE RATIOS ACCORDINGLY

MEASURING PERFORMANCE

STOCK DAYS

	Step 1 Establish Daily Usage		Step 2 Calculate No. Days Stock
RAW MATERIAL	£ Planned Material Issues / No. of Days plan covers	= →	£ Stock of Raw Materials / £ Av. Daily Issues
WORK IN PROGRESS	£ Planned Completed Prodn / No. of Days plan covers	= →	£ Stock of Work in Progress / £ Av. Daily Completed Prodn
FINISHED GOODS	£ Planned Cost of Goods Sold / No. of Days plan covers	= →	£ Stock of finished Goods / £ Av. Daily Cost of Goods

MANAGING WORKING CAPITAL

MEASURING PERFORMANCE
DEBTOR/CREDITOR DAYS

No. days Debtors $=$ $\dfrac{\text{£ Debtors}}{\text{£ Credit Sales per day}}$

No. days Creditors $=$ $\dfrac{\text{£ Creditors}}{\text{£ Purchases per day}}$

The advantages of using these ratios are:

1   They are user-friendly; most people can identify with the concept of measuring 'days in stock', etc

2   They are not distorted by changes in the level of activity

Note: Exclude cash sales and purchases which clearly do not relate to Debtors/Creditors

MEASURING PERFORMANCE

INTERPRETATION

However

- Interpret the 'days' with caution

- 20 days' Raw Material stock does not mean you can stop all deliveries and continue to issue to Work in Progress for 20 days without shortages

  - stock is unlikely to be in the proportions required (ie: you may have 30 days' stock of some components, 10 of others)

  - no allowance is made in the calculation for slow-moving or redundant stock

- Debtor days will vary by customer

- Creditor days will vary by supplier

REDUCING WORKING CAPITAL

There are two ways to reduce Working Capital:

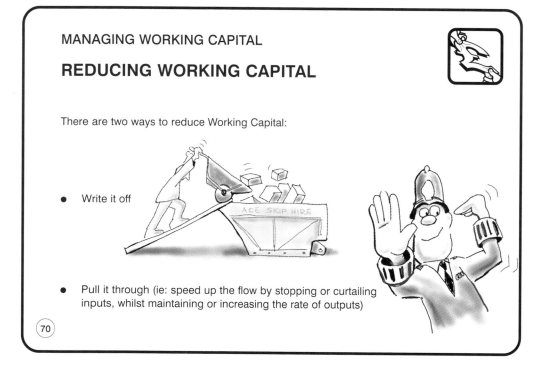

- Write it off

- Pull it through (ie: speed up the flow by stopping or curtailing inputs, whilst maintaining or increasing the rate of outputs)

REDUCING WORKING CAPITAL
WRITE-OFFS

- Writing it off, eg:
  - Redundant Materials
  - Bad Debts

Financial implications:

Cash	-	Nil effect (other than, eg: scrap value for redundant material)
Profit this year	-	Reduced by the amount of the write-off
	-	Enhanced by savings in space and activity costs (eg: Redundant Material Storage)
Profit in subsequent years	-	Enhanced by savings in space and activity costs
Working Capital	-	Reduced for this and subsequent years by the amount written off
Return in subsequent years	-	Improves due to reduced investment in working capital and cost savings

REDUCING WORKING CAPITAL

MAKING WRITE-OFFS

- **Stock:**

Examine all stock for:

Redundancy - due to, eg: ◆ modifications ◆ customer cancellations
◆ surplus stockholding ◆ damage

Realisability - stock must be valued at the **lower** of cost
and net realisable value

Write off already redundant stock and make reserves for stock likely to become redundant

- **Debtors:**

Write-off bad debts and make provisions where there is some doubt that the debt
will be collected

Note: *Accountants should already be doing this to produce their published accounts!*

REDUCING WORKING CAPITAL
PULLING IT THROUGH

- Drive out surplus investment by:
  - reducing days spent in Raw Materials
  - reduced lead time through the shopfloor
  - reducing days spent in Finished Goods
  - reducing days credit given to customers

Financial implications:

Cash	-	As investment in Stock and Debtors is reduced, there will be a once-off increase in cash
Profit	-	Enhanced this year and subsequent years by savings in space and activity costs ... and reduced risk (page 62)
Working Capital	-	Reduced this and subsequent years by the investment released

Note: *Do not underestimate the time required to achieve this benefit!* *- see page 90.*
If the process can be continued less cash will be required to finance growth.

DRIVE OUT SURPLUS INVESTMENT
STOCK: CAUSAL ANALYSIS

A successful campaign to permanently eliminate surplus Working Capital requires each of the components of the cycle to be examined in turn.

Stock

- Carry out a **Causal Analysis**
  - *Why does the business hold stock?*
    'Our customers demand immediate delivery'
    'Our customers demand lead times which are shorter than
       our production lead times'
    'Demand for our product is seasonal'
    'We cannot eliminate production bottlenecks'
    'We cannot rely on our suppliers', etc, etc

- To eliminate stock permanently these **Causal Factors** must be challenged and changed
- Without this, any reduction in stock will be short-term as the **Causal Factors** will drive the stock up again

DRIVE OUT SURPLUS INVESTMENT
STOCK FLOW

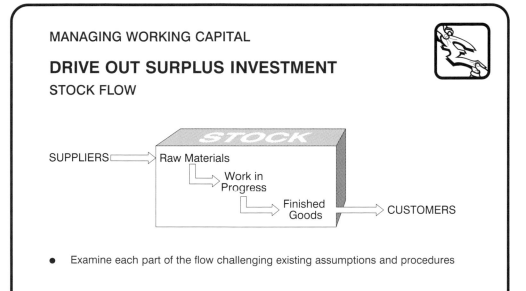

- Examine each part of the flow challenging existing assumptions and procedures

DRIVE OUT SURPLUS INVESTMENT
STOCK: TO STORES

Suppliers ⟶ Raw Material Stores

Manage the supplier partnership professionally!

There are many 'win win' strategies!
Could you:

- Improve production scheduling
- Rationalise suppliers and use enhanced purchasing power to reduce prices
  (which reduces stock values, releases cash and improves profit)
- Plan and negotiate Just In Time (JIT) deliveries for fast moving stocks
  (and use up current stocks before implementation)
- Negotiate with Suppliers to reduce lead times and/or to hold buffer stocks for you
- Negotiate with Suppliers for consignment stock to be held (ie: suppliers' stock
  held on your premises for you to call off as required)
- Manage imported items carefully - use bonded stores / import agents
- Give special attention to high unit value purchases

DRIVE OUT SURPLUS INVESTMENT
STOCK: TO STORES

Suppliers ———→ Raw Material Stores

Could you:

- Review order quantities
- Buy in kits, rather than kit parts, yourself
- Buy in sub-assemblies, rather than assemble parts yourself
- Review and challenge the batch size
- Balance production weekly to avoid month end peaks

- Avoid the common weakness of deliveries in the last week of the month for use the following month

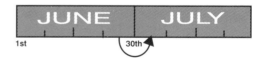

Schedule deliveries to the beginning of the month (where appropriate) - (reduces stock, releases cash and can extend credit from suppliers for an additional 30 days)

DRIVE OUT SURPLUS INVESTMENT

STOCK: TO FINISHED GOODS

Raw Materials ⟶ WIP ⟶ Finished Goods

Could you:

- Improve production scheduling and move towards JIT

- Identify production bottle-necks and challenge those processes

- Speed up process time by reviewing process organisation:
  - on site: the layout of the materials flow around the site; consider cellular organisation to reduce the distance and release the stock
  - between sites: map flow of products between sites and/or sub-contractors; minimise 'Motorway Stocks'!

- Avoid Free Issue of materials to Sub-Contractors; Sub-Contractors should order direct - if this is not possible then sell the items to the Sub-Contractor

MANAGING WORKING CAPITAL

DRIVE OUT SURPLUS INVESTMENT
STOCK: TO CUSTOMERS

Finished Goods Stores ⟶ Customers

Could you:

- Identify all obsolete stock and sell off as spares - or for scrap

- Review lead times quoted to customers and hence finished goods stockholding policies

DRIVE OUT SURPLUS INVESTMENT
STOCK: GENERAL

- Improve Sales Forecasting techniques - poor forecasting results in stock problems

- Rationalise the range of finished products

- Rationalise the range of components - move towards common parts

- Use 80/20 rule - focus on the 20% key items which result in 80% of the stock value

- New products and product modifications - assess implications of lead times and existing stock holding

- Plan marketing initiatives, eg: promotions
  - how much extra stock is required? ... and WHEN?
  - what will be done with surplus stock?

DRIVE OUT SURPLUS INVESTMENT
DEBTORS: CAUSAL ANALYSIS

Who's to blame?

- Do not make the mistake of
  assuming all late payments
  from customers are due to
  lazy/inefficient accountants!

- A **Causal Analysis** of overdue
  payments can be revealing;
  do any of the following apply to your business?

  Causal Factors:
  Product rejected - poor quality
  Inadequate paperwork
  Incorrect paperwork
  Wrong delivery point
  Not delivered in accordance with customer's schedule

DRIVE OUT SURPLUS INVESTMENT
DEBTORS: CREDIT TERMS

Customers don't 'take' credit; you MANAGE it!

- Negotiate and agree credit terms

- Agree a basis for invoicing part-deliveries

- Are stage payments appropriate?

- Apply effective credit control:
    - establish an accurate reporting system, eg: Ageing Analysis
    - provide Sales with such reports
    - monitor future deliveries and, if necessary,
    - put customer on STOP

- Ensure those negotiating sales understand the trade-off for your business between Price and Credit given and **know the cost of credit!**

DRIVE OUT SURPLUS INVESTMENT
DEBTORS: INVOICE ACCURACY

Get the invoice right!

- Ensure the invoice is accurate

- Quote the items specified by the customer on the invoice, eg:
  - order number
  - test report, etc

- Send the invoice to the correct address, which is not necessarily the delivery address

- Ensure support reports specified by the Customer (eg: Quality Reports, Test Reports, etc) are forwarded with the invoice

DRIVE OUT SURPLUS INVESTMENT
DEBTORS: ADMIN ACCURACY

Get the admin right!

- Nurse the debt!
- Understand your customers' procedures and the personnel involved in processing and paying your invoice
- For significant sales 'nurse' the invoice through the system identifying and resolving issues **before** the debt is overdue
    - have the goods been received?
    - have they passed inspection?
    - has the invoice been cleared?

- Ensure invoices are posted promptly
- Ensure a control process is in place to trigger invoices for Stage Payments
- Identify responsibility for credit control

MANAGING WORKING CAPITAL

DRIVE OUT SURPLUS INVESTMENT
DEBTORS: TIMING

Beware the Hockey stick!

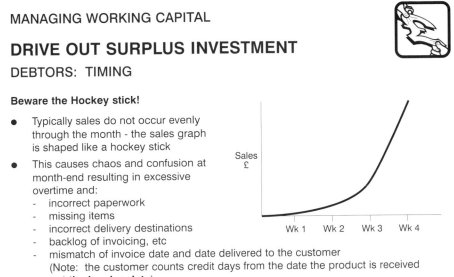

- Typically sales do not occur evenly through the month - the sales graph is shaped like a hockey stick

- This causes chaos and confusion at month-end resulting in excessive overtime and:
  - incorrect paperwork
  - missing items
  - incorrect delivery destinations
  - backlog of invoicing, etc
  - mismatch of invoice date and date delivered to the customer
    (Note: the customer counts credit days from the date the product is received **not the invoice date**)

  ... all of which lead to delayed payments by customers

MANAGING WORKING CAPITAL

DRIVE OUT SURPLUS INVESTMENT

CASH

- Cash forms part of the Working Capital cycle, and hence every £1 is represented by £1 Capital Employed

- Whilst a business should aim to have sufficient cash to meet its needs, surplus cash lying idle - or invested at a relatively low rate of return - will depress R.O.C.E. (Return on Capital Employed)

- Measures of cash levels (Liquidity Ratios) are explained in Appendix Two

DRIVE OUT SURPLUS INVESTMENT
CREDITORS: PARTNERSHIP

- The situation here is different as, by increasing the amount of credit taken from suppliers, the company's investment in Working Capital is reduced

However

- Suppliers are part of the team and therefore credit taken should be a matter of negotiation - not unilateral action!

- Without the benefits of partnerships with suppliers, how will the business achieve its other drives:
  - deliveries direct to line   - improved quality; zero defects, etc
  - reduced lead times?

- The supplier can also **win** in the partnership
  - supplier rationalisation ('Preferred Supplier' status)
  - guarantees of workload

MANAGING WORKING CAPITAL

DRIVE OUT SURPLUS INVESTMENT
CREDITORS: INVOICES

Choosing Suppliers

- Criteria should include a test of financial viability
  - avoid suppliers who cannot honour agreed terms

Credit to run from Receipt of Goods

- Avoid progress payments - particularly on expensive capital items; negotiate price and payment terms before placing the order

- Imported Goods? Try to avoid Letters of Credit; negotiate credit period from delivery to site **NOT** date of despatch - why not source locally if possible?

- Under-delivery? Advise supplier that credit will run from the date of completed delivery

- Schedule deliveries at the beginning of the month rather than the end of the preceding month (see page 77)

DRIVE OUT SURPLUS INVESTMENT
CREDITORS: ADMIN

Problem with the invoice?

- Disputed invoices should be held until a credit note is received or the issue resolved

- Incorrect invoices should be returned to the supplier for replacement

Cleared for payment?

- Set up a monthly payment run, ie: one cheque run per month

- Introduce an Age Analysis to ensure suppliers are not paid prior to the agreed dates

    - beware informal relationships with suppliers!

DRIVE OUT SURPLUS INVESTMENT

TIMESCALE

- Whilst it is important to initiate action, do not underestimate the timescales required to achieve the benefits

- For example:

  It is usually impractical to 'turn the tap off' from suppliers completely

  i) Stocks will not necessarily be available in the required proportions

  ii) What effect would this have on the suppliers, and the supplier/customer relationship?

  Reducing purchases will not have an immediate effect on cash or working capital if credit is normally given by the supplier, as previous months' supplies will still become due for payment

- The process requires careful planning of the levels of input and output from each component of the cycle until an efficient equilibrium is reached

MANAGING WORKING CAPITAL

DRIVE OUT SURPLUS INVESTMENT
MOVING TOWARDS J.I.T.

Beware!

- The process of going JIT entails driving out existing stock and only manufacturing the balancing amount required to meet demand

- In the initial stages, therefore, manufacturing will be at a level below normal demand

- The effect of this is a short-term profit drop as the period's results bear the brunt of the previously stocked overheads and the relatively high overhead cost per unit of the low volume manufacturing

- This problem remains until capacity, demand and output are in equilibrium

SUMMARY

Managing Working Capital requires a planned progression through the cycle back into cash.

There are various targets/meetings to measure this progress, but all are subordinate to **CASH**.

SUMMARY

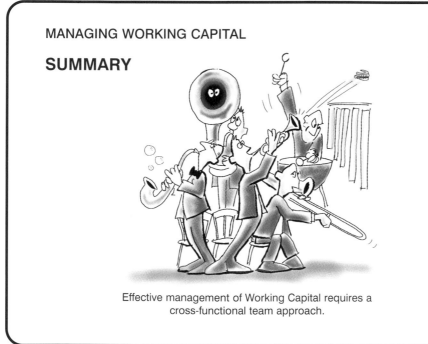

Effective management of Working Capital requires a
cross-functional team approach.

SUMMARY

DON'T TRY TO DO IT BY YOURSELF!

APPENDICES

JARGON EXPLAINED

GLOSSARY OF TERMS

JARGON EXPLAINED

GLOSSARY OF TERMS

		Page
Dividend:	The part of **Earnings** paid out to the Shareholders in order to give them an income on their investment	51
Earnings:	The profits left for the shareholders once all the business costs (including **Interest** and **Tax**) have been met. Some will be paid out as **Dividend**, the rest reinvested - **Retained Profit**	51
Factoring:	Selling **Debtors** to a third party at a discount, for cash	12
Fixed Assets:	Facilities or Processes providing the infrastructure of the business. These are purchased for use within the business rather than for purposes of re-sale	58
Interest:	Lenders will expect a return on their investment in the form of interest	47
Liquidation:	Winding up of a business - often due to an inability to pay its debts	5
Liquidity:	Ability to pay debts as they become due	102

APPENDIX ONE

JARGON EXPLAINED

GLOSSARY OF TERMS

APPENDIX ONE

JARGON EXPLAINED

GLOSSARY OF TERMS

		Page
ROCE:	Return on Capital Employed. Measures the effective use of **Net Capital Employed** to generate **Operating Profit**	86
	$$= \frac{\textbf{Operating Profit}}{\textbf{Net Capital Employed}} \times 100$$	
Sales:	The invoice value of goods sold (excluding VAT)	18
Share Capital:	Long-term funding by shareholders who buy a share of the business	54
Stock:	The total value of raw materials, work in progress and finished goods	59
Tax:	Part of company profits have to be used to finance the tax bill	50
Working Capital:	Funds used to provide the flow of materials, services and credit. (**Current Assets - Current Liabilities**)	59

LIQUIDITY RATIOS

The objective of Liquidity Ratios is to monitor the perceived **THREAT** from current liabilities:

- What if the bank calls in the overdraft?

- What if suppliers demand payment? etc

APPENDIX TWO

LIQUIDITY RATIOS

Current Ratio	Current Assets : Current Liabilities
Acid Test Ratio	(Current Assets - Stocks): Current Liabilities This more stringent ratio excludes stocks on the basis that they take time to convert into cash

- These ratios should not be used blindly!

- Think about how the Working Capital cycle operates in your particular business and remember that what you are trying to assess is your business's ability to meet the current liabilities as and when they fall due

LIQUIDITY RATIOS

- Look at the liquidity/risk specific to your business: consider each element
  of the cycle

  Stock: How liquid is it?

  Remember it must also pass through Debtors before becoming Cash

  Food Retailing: - short time on shelf and cash sales

  ⟶ **Highly liquid**

  Ship-building: - long lead-time and extended credit

  ⟶ **Not liquid**

  Debtors: How quickly will these be paid? 30 days? 60 days? Extended credit?

  Current
  Liabilities: When will each type of payment fall due?

  Suppliers - 30 days? 60 days?

  Bank Overdraft - subject to call at short notice from bank

  Tax/Dividend - on specific dates

PROFIT TO CASH RECONCILIATION
WORKED EXAMPLE

PRINNY PLC

Prepare a Profit to Cash Reconciliation for the 3 months ended 31st March 200-

Basic information:

- Customers have 2 months' credit

- Material suppliers are paid 2 months after the goods are received

- Wages and overheads are paid as incurred

- Depreciation for the period is £10k

- Materials are purchased the month prior to use in production

- Products are manufactured in the month prior to sale

PROFIT TO CASH RECONCILIATION

PRINNY PLC

- Other information:

	Nov £k	Dec £k	Jan £k	Feb £k	Mar £k
Sales	100	120	150	150	130
Materials Received	45	45	39	48	45
Wages & Overheads	70	75	75	65	80

PROFIT TO CASH RECONCILIATION

PRINNY PLC

Profit and Loss Account for the 3 months ended 31st March 200-		
	£k	£k
Sales		430 **ⓐ**
Cost of Sales:		
Materials	129 **ⓑ**	
Wages & Overheads	215 **ⓒ**	
Depreciation	10	
		354
Operating Profit		76
Interest paid	5	
Tax paid	15	
		20
Earnings		56
Dividend paid		20
Retained Profit		36 **ⓜ**

PROFIT TO CASH RECONCILIATION

PRINNY PLC

Balance Sheet as at		1.1.200-			31.3.200-	
	£k	£k	£k	£k	£k	£k
Fixed Assets			200 **k**			250 **k**
Current Assets:						
Stock		165 **d**			173 **g**	
Debtors		220 **e**			280 **h**	
Cash		50			-	
		435			453	
Current Liabilities:						
Creditors	90 **f**			93 **j**		
Bank o/draft	-	90		9		
					102	
Working Capital			345			351
Net Assets Employed			545			601
Share Capital		100			100	
Reserves		245 **m**			281 **m**	
Net Worth			345			381
Loans			200			220
Net Capital Employed			545			601

PROFIT TO CASH RECONCILIATION

Note: **a** to **j**

Figures on the statement can be traced back to the basic information:

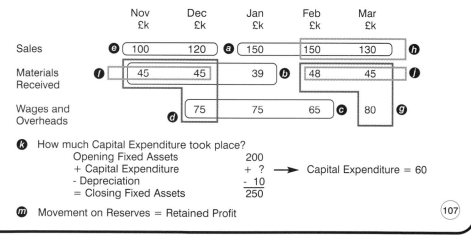

	Nov £k	Dec £k	Jan £k	Feb £k	Mar £k
Sales	**e** 100	120	**a** 150	150	130 **h**
Materials Received	**f** 45	45	39 **b**	48	45 **i**
Wages and Overheads		**d** 75	75	65 **c**	80 **g**

k How much Capital Expenditure took place?

Opening Fixed Assets	200
+ Capital Expenditure	+ ?
− Depreciation	− 10
= Closing Fixed Assets	250

→ Capital Expenditure = 60

m Movement on Reserves = Retained Profit

PROFIT TO CASH RECONCILIATION

PRINNY PLC

Profit to Cash Reconciliation for the 3 months ended 31st March 200-		
		Workings
Operating Profit	76	*See P & L Account*
Add back: Depreciation	10	*Ref Basic Information*
Increase in Stock	(8)	*Ref Balance Sheet (173-165) = (8)*
Increase in Debtors	(60)	*Ref Balance Sheet (280-220) = (60)*
Increase in Creditors	3	*Ref Balance Sheet (93-90) = 3*
Interest paid	(5)	}
Dividend paid	(20)	} *See P & L Account*
Tax paid	(15)	}
Capital Expenditure	(60)	*Ref note* **k**
Increase in Loans	20	*Ref Balance Sheet (220-200) = 20*
Net Cashflow	(59)	
Opening Cash	50	
Closing (Bank overdraft)	(9)	
(Decrease) in Cash	(59)	

About the Authors

Anne Hawkins, BA, ACMA is a Management Accountant with a first class honours degree in Business Studies. Anne has progressed from this strong knowledge base to gain senior management accounting experience within consumer and industrial product industries. As a Training Consultant she develops and presents finance programmes to Directors and Managers from all sections of industry.

Clive Turner, ACMA, MBCS is Managing Director of Structured Learning Programmes Ltd, established in 1981 to provide management consultancy and training services. Clive works with management to develop strategic business options. He participates in the evaluation process: designs the appropriate organisation structure and provides management development to support the implementation process. Clive continues to have extensive experience in delivering financial modules within Masters Programmes in the UK and overseas.

Contact

For details of support materials available to help trainers and managers run finance courses in-company, contact the authors at:
Clive: Tall Trees, Barkers Lane, Wythall, West Midlands B47 6BS.
Anne: The Spinney, 27 Queens Road, Cheltenham GL50 2LX.

© Anne Hawkins and Clive Turner 1995
This edition published in 1995 by Management Pocketbooks Ltd.
Laurel House, Station Approach, Alresford, Hants SO24 9JH, U.K.

Reprinted 1997, 2000, 2002, 2004.   Printed in UK   ISBN 1 870471 33 4

Your details

Name

Position

Company

Address

Telephone

Facsimile

E-mail

VAT No. (EC companies)

Your Order Ref

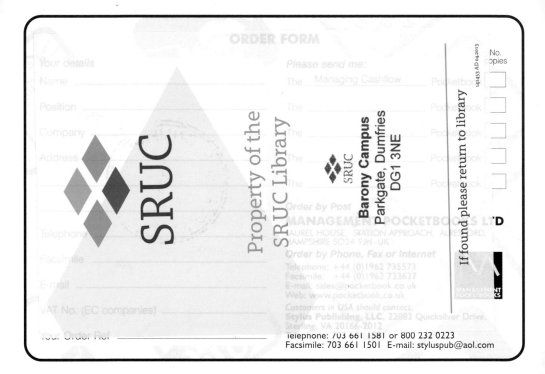

Please send me:

		No. copies
The	Managing Cashflow	Pocketbook
The		Pocketbook
The		Pocketbook
The		Pocketbook
The		Pocketbook

141453 AD 04.2013

Order by Post
MANAGEMENT POCKETBOOKS LTD
LAUREL HOUSE, STATION APPROACH, ALRESFORD,
HAMPSHIRE SO24 9JH UK

Order by Phone, Fax or Internet
Telephone: +44 (0)1962 735573
Facsimile: +44 (0)1962 733637
E-mail: sales@pocketbook.co.uk
Web: www.pocketbook.co.uk

Customers in USA should contact:
Stylus Publishing, LLC, 22883 Quicksilver Drive,
Sterling, VA 20166-2012
Telephone: 703 661 1581 or 800 232 0223
Facsimile: 703 661 1501 E-mail: styluspub@aol.com